I0845498

JACK AND THE FARMER

BY

DONNA WEBERNICK

JACK AND THE FARMER

BY
DONNA WEBERNICK

ALL GRAPHICS WERE TAKEN FROM
CANVA AND MADE INTO MY DESIGN

Dear Reader,

Thank you for purchasing Jack and The Farmer. I hope you enjoy reading it as much as I enjoyed writing it.

Best Regards,
DONNA WEBERNICK

A rabbit named Jack lived on
a farm with cows, chickens,
pigs, and a farmer named Al.

"He would follow Farmer Al all around the farm as he performed his daily chores."

Farmer Al gave him fresh lettuce daily to lead him to the garden.

Jack would follow the helpers on the farm, hoping to get fresh milk.

"He enjoyed watching them feed
the chickens."

Jack saw Mr. Mike picking corn and hopped over to see him. Mr. Mike would laugh every time he saw the little rabbit.

Jack visited Mr. Bill daily
while he fed the pigs.

Next, Jack approaches Farmer Al's wife, Lisa, to observe her tending to her prize-winning tomatoes.

Jack enjoyed receiving a daily carrot or two from the farmers during harvest.

Every time Jack saw the tractor,
he would hide because he was
frightened by the noise it made
as the farmer drove by.

Jack came across Peter watering the plants and thought he would stop by for a drink. Peter laughed at Jack and said, "You must be thirsty from hopping from place to place." He then gave Jack a drink of water.

After Jack had finished his water,
he saw Mr. McGregor bringing hay
to Farmer Al.

Mr. McGregor greeted Al, "Hi Al, I
see you still have Jack."
"Oh yes, he follows me everywhere
I go," Farmer Al replied. Mr.
McGregor just laughed.

Jack saw Joe passing by and pushed him to the barn in the wheelbarrow while moving the pumpkins from the garden to the barn.

While Joe was unloading the
pumpkins, Jack found the hay so
inviting that he decided to lie down
for a short nap.

When Jack woke up from his nap, he heard the sound of laughter. The children were outside playing and working. They were both delighted to see their little furry friend.

Ms. Barb said, " Hi, Jack. What took you so long to see me today? Unfortunately, I have nothing for you to eat, but I am happy to see you."

Ms. Mindy spotted Jack and offered him an apple. He nibbled it to the core, and she chuckled, "You must have been a starving rabbit, Jack."

There is a farmers' market on Saturdays, and Jack enjoys watching all the people who come to buy. Sometimes, they even give him something to eat.

Bell, the farmer's cat, enjoys playing with Jack but usually sleeps in the house.

Jack enjoys the aroma of blooming
flowers. He likes to sit on the soil
beneath them to cool off from the
scorching sun.

Life is busy for Jack on the farm.
He is exhausted and ready for a
good night's sleep.

Jack's job on the farm is to visit
and eat.

After a good night's sleep, Jack goes on daily rounds at the farm to visit all the workers. He leads a busy life as a farm rabbit.